S0-ATR-986

THE LITTLE
CAT CARE
Book

ELIZABETH MARTYN
DAVID TAYLOR
Photography by Jane Burton

DORLING KINDERSLEY, INC.
New York

A DORLING KINDERSLEY BOOK

EDITOR Jane Mason

ART EDITOR Lee Griffiths

MANAGING EDITOR Krystyna Mayer

MANAGING ART EDITOR Derek Coombes

PRODUCTION Hilary Stephens

First American Edition, 1991
10 9 8 7 6 5 4 3 2 1

Dorling Kindersley, Inc., 232 Madison Avenue
New York, New York 10016

Copyright © 1991 Dorling Kindersley Limited, London
Text copyright © 1991 Elizabeth Martyn and David Taylor

All rights reserved under International and Pan-American Copyright
Conventions. Published in the United States by Dorling Kindersley, Inc.,
New York, New York. Distributed by Houghton Mifflin Company,
Boston, Massachusetts. First published in Great Britain by Dorling
Kindersley Limited, London. No part of this publication may be
reproduced, stored in a retrieval system, or transmitted in any form or by
any means, electronic, mechanical, photocopying, recording, or
otherwise, without the prior written permission of the copyright owner.

ISBN 1-879431-62-9
Library of Congress Catalog Card Number 91-072735

Reproduced by Colourscan, Singapore
Printed and bound in Hong Kong by Imago

CONTENTS

HAPPY

Cats

*Body language, vocal
clues, and everyday
behavior provide
valuable insights into
your cat's feelings.*

PAMPERED CATS

Throughout history, tradition has decreed that cats be a pampered, even venerated, species.

The tradition of treating cats lavishly began with the ancient Egyptians. A magnificent red granite temple was built on the banks of the Nile River, and dedicated to Bastet the ruling cat goddess. Cats inspired similar respect in Japan, where they were declared sacred around 1000 A.D. For centuries cats were kept in the lap of luxury.

CARING FOR CATS

At the death of a beloved Egyptian domestic cat, the family shaved off their eyebrows as a sign of deep mourning. After an elaborate funeral, those cats belonging to especially wealthy owners were buried in jeweled caskets, with a generous supply of mummified rats and mice for nourishment in the afterworld.

The Prophet Mohammed cut off the sleeve of his robe rather than disturb his sleeping cat. Missionary Albert Schweitzer, who was left-handed, would write laboriously with his right hand in order not to waken his pet, Sizi, who liked to curl up for a nap in the crook of his left arm. Sir Isaac Newton, famous pioneer of the sciences, is also credited with the invention of the cat door or cat flap. He cut two holes, one for his favorite cat and another, smaller one, for her litter of young kittens.

CLASSY CATS

Memorable examples of top cats are Hamlet, resident of the Algonquin Hotel in New York;

Left: Bathtime babies
Above: Mischief with the hatbox
Right: An Egyptian lady mourns her pet cat

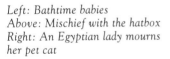

or royal cats such as White Heather, Queen Victoria's pretty Persian. The Earl of Chesterfield left generous pensions to his cats when he died in 1773. Lucky cats in America and Britain have inherited up to $4 million.

FAMOUS CATS

Cats have been the chosen companions to generations of the great and the good, the rich, and the famous.

Their languorous elegance delights artists, their discretion appeals to politicians, and their totally uninhibited behavior inspires writers. American Presidents and British Prime Ministers have shared a great affection for cats.

CATS IN POLITICS

Jock, Winston Churchill's ginger cat, slept on his master's bed; later, Nemu the Siamese moved into No. 10 with Harold Wilson. Wilberforce was well known as cat-in-residence at Downing Street under four Prime Ministers. Policemen on duty outside No. 10 rang the doorbell when Wilberforce wanted to go in. The Roosevelt family also loved cats. Slippers, one White House resident, was known to appear at many state occasions. Another, Tom Quartz, had his own biography written.

CATS IN LITERATURE

Many a famous writer has been grateful for the companionship of a faithful cat. Edgar Allan Poe worked best with his cat perched on his shoulder. Amazingly, Ernest Hemingway did complete one of his novels in the company of no less than 34 cats. Charles Dickens often gave cats bit parts in his novels. He owned a white cat called William, whose party trick was snuffing out the candle with his paw. The Brontë sisters, who lived in an isolated Yorkshire parsonage, enjoyed the company of cats, and wrote sadly to close

Left: Actress Hayley Mills and contented feline friend
Right: Humphrey, a notable cat at No. 10 Downing Street
Below: Space cat Jones with Sigourney Weaver

friends to pass on the news when one very much-loved pet, called Tiger, died.

CATS IN THE MOVIES

Cats, as sensuous or sinister symbols, have made memorable appearances in films as diverse as *Breakfast at Tiffany's*, *The Incredible Journey*, *La Dolce Vita*, *Diamonds Are Forever* (which features Solomon, an unblinking white chinchilla), and *Alien*. But perhaps the best recent celebration of cats has been Andrew Lloyd Webber's smash hit musical, *Cats*.

Is your Cat Happy?

Your cat has an infinite variety of ways to tell you when all's right in the feline world. Ears pricked up and held forward show that your cat is alert and interested in what's going on. Whiskers pointing out to the sides of the face, neither bunched nor fanned out, mean puss is feeling calm and comfortable. A straight tail raised aloft is a way of saying "Hello." A quick flip of the tail tip is another greeting sign.

Trusting Friend
A confident cat rolls over, displaying his abdomen. A cat who is less sure flops down at your feet for a stroke.

Perfect Pleasure
Purring is the ultimate expression of delight. The louder the purr, the happier the cat.

LITTLE GESTURES

Rubbing around your legs is a reminder that it's feeding time. Your cat is also marking you as feline property, using scent glands beneath the chin and forehead.

WONDERFUL WELCOME

A little hop, with both front paws raised a few inches from the ground, sometimes accompanied by a little chirping cry, is an affectionate greeting used by cats pleased to see their owners.

FOND MEMORIES

When your cat leaps on to your lap and tramples your thighs with insistent paws, she is remembering the blissful days of kittenhood. Tiny kittens pummel their mother's belly to stimulate the flow of milk, and this habit is often retained in adult life.

Is your Cat Unhappy?

If your cat is frightened or angry, all the clues are there to see. The pupils are enlarged, the ears held flat against the head, and the tail beats on the ground.

Sounds of Protest

A high-pitched mew given by kittens is their only way of telling their mother that they are lost, cold, or frightened. The mew gets louder and more strident if the kitten is losing a battle with one of his siblings. Adult cats use a short, high-pitched "meow" to tell you that something is wrong. This is the cry you will also hear when your cat is shut in a room and wants to be let out at once. A cat who is feeling puzzled and unhappy gives a couple of quick tongue flicks over the lips. This is often the response to a particularly irritating noise.

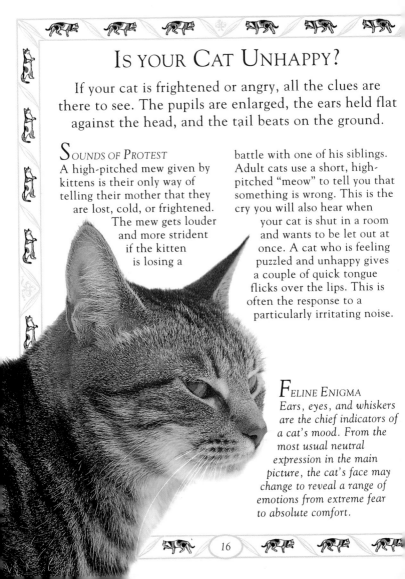

Feline Enigma

Ears, eyes, and whiskers are the chief indicators of a cat's mood. From the most usual neutral expression in the main picture, the cat's face may change to reveal a range of emotions from extreme fear to absolute comfort.

ATTACK ALERT

Most owners have seen their pet come face to face with the neighborhood bully on the garden fence. The cat's ears turn back, and the head sways from side to side, with eyes fixed on the enemy. The whiskers fan out, showing that action is imminent. The cat arches his back, and a band of fur stands up along his spine.

TROUBLED TABBY

A cat who has suddenly taken fright at an unexpected noise will crouch low, ready to flee.

WATCHING AND WAITING

A cat poised with front legs straight and back legs bent is expressing uncertainty about what to do next. If the forelegs are also bent, and the cat is crouching, there's no doubt that danger is just around the corner. Rapid twitching of the ears is a sure sign of a cat who's feeling a trifle nervous. Watch your cat's ears next time you have to scold him.

ANXIOUS MOMENTS

Fur standing on end and ears flicked back show that this young cat is getting worried. Her tail is looped into the classic "witch's cat" position.

THE CAT FOR YOUR LIFESTYLE

Selecting the right cat to share your life isn't just a
matter of picking the most appealing kitten in the
litter. First you must decide what kind of cat would fit
best into your world. Do you want an indoor cat, or
will your new friend be free to roam? How much time
can you spend with your cat – if the answer is very
little, why not get two cats as companions for each
other? And can you cope with a kitten, or
would an adult be a better choice?

THE PERFECT PET

As a very general rule, pedigree
longhaired cats tend to be more
placid by nature, and happier
to stay at home than pedigree
shorthaired, and particularly
Oriental, breeds. However,
you must have the time to
spend on grooming. Some
Oriental cats, like the
Siamese and Burmese,
crave company even
though they also need
freedom. Kittens need
extra care and can be very
demanding. Neutered males
and females are equally sociable.

ALL-ROUND WINNER
The domestic non-pedigree is a robust cat, who adapts well to the rigors of family life.

CHARISMATIC CAT
Choose a regal Abyssinian for its boundless energy and superb good looks.

FRIENDLY GIANT
The tolerant and affectionate Maine Coon grows to a most impressive size.

HEALTHY
Cats

All you need to know about health, fitness, and grooming to keep your cat up to scratch.

Choosing a Cat or Kitten

When you come to choose a cat or kitten, there are lots of important questions to bear in mind, from coat and color, to behavior and breed.

Kitten or Cat?

First decide whether you want a kitten or an adult cat. For the first couple of months, kittens need three meals a day and as much time as you can give them. Kittens are boisterous, so opt for a more sedate, older cat if you have a lot of treasures, or furniture that won't stand up to rough treatment. Before you bring your new cat home, make sure that a kitten has been given essential vaccinations, and that adults are up to date on boosters and have been neutered, unless you want to breed them, of course.

Character Cat
This young adult cat is alert, bright-eyed, and healthy.

The best place to get a cat or kitten is from someone you know, through a humane society, or from a breeder. Here's what to look for:

1 Kittens should be playful and active. Encourage an older cat to jump or run to show that movement is easy.

2 Eyes should be bright, teeth sound, ears and nose clean. There should be no sign of an upset stomach.

3 The coat should be glossy and well cared for. Ruffle the fur backward to search for telltale black specks left by fleas.

4 Choose a cat that is inquisitive and responds happily to being stroked and handled.

5 Longhairs demand time and patience for daily grooming sessions. Think carefully before making this commitment!

Ragdoll Charmer
This little kitten displays the gentle demeanor that makes the breed so sought after.

Fluffy Friend
Often docile by nature, longhairs are loyal and loving companions.

KITTEN CARE

Moving into a new home is a big adventure for a little
kitten, and one that should not be undertaken until
puss is at least eight to ten weeks old.

FIRST THINGS FIRST
Before you bring your kitten
home, make a few preparations.
Kittens need a bed of their
own, lined with a warm,
washable blanket, personal
bowls for food and water and,
of course, a litter box.

LESSONS FOR LIFE
Give your kitten lots of
affection. Welcome her onto
your lap, and pick her up if she
cries for attention. Don't be
too soft though. It's never too
soon to start teaching that "no"
definitely means "NO!"

HELP!
Ginger is only six weeks
old when she first meets
a young pup – and she is
just a bit scared.

BEST FRIENDS
Soon puppy and kitten are playing together happily. Careful early introductions make for lasting friendships.

TRAINING TECHNIQUES

How much you can train your cat to do depends on how willing your cat is to be trained! To achieve the best results, start early, and be patient but persistent.

LEADING THE WAY

Many cats are happy to walk on a leash. Start training in kittenhood, letting your cat get used to wearing the leash without you holding it. Give short training sessions, indoors at first. Don't drag at the leash: use gentle encouragement with lots of reassuring words. Only venture outside when your cat is completely used to walking with you.

WALKIES!

Siamese and other Oriental cats enjoy walking on a leash.

IN AND OUT

If you buy a cat door for your pet, make sure that you choose one that has a lock or closure for nighttime security.

FELINE FREEDOM

Both cats and owners appreciate the advantages of a cat flap, which allows your pet to come and go freely. Some cats take to them immediately, while others find them puzzling and even frightening. If your cat seems confused, try propping the flap open for a day or two, so that she gets used to hopping through the gap. Then try closing the flap and calling her name, or rattling a food bowl from the other side as an extra incentive. Cats are clever creatures and soon work out just what to do.

LITTER LESSONS

Cats are instinctively clean and quickly learn to use a litter box, which should always be kept in the same place to avoid mistakes and confusion. Keep the litter box clean and wipe up any mishaps with mild bleach, *never* ammonia.

GOOD HABITS

Pop your kitten into the box after meals. In a day or two she will know the routine.

COAT CARE

There's no getting away from it: daily grooming is vital for many cats. Make it a pleasure rather than a 'chore – your cat will thoroughly enjoy your undivided attention and you'll be rewarded by the glorious sight of your glamorous pet.

LONGHAIRED LOVELY
A contented cat, freshly groomed to fluffy perfection.

TANGLE FREE
Work methodically to remove knots. If your cat roams outside, you will probably find burrs and bits of twig caught in the coat.

ESSENTIAL EQUIPMENT

A bristle brush is kind to the coat and good for all-over brushing. Use a wire slicker brush to work through the length of the fur. Combs with wide and narrow teeth are useful for teasing out knots and tangles. Cotton swabs come in handy for cleaning the ears, but balls are safer when cleansing around the eyes. A soft toothbrush is ideal for gently teasing out the fur around the face and on the chest and legs. A soft cloth is often used for polishing the coats of shorthaired cats.

Grooming Shorthairs

Shorthaired cats make a good job of grooming themselves, but to keep them in top condition, they need regular brush-and-comb sessions to keep their coats glossy, smooth, and absolutely free of tangles.

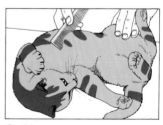

Warning Signs

Black specks in the coat mean fleas. To check, wipe them on a moist tissue – if they are flea droppings, they will leave a dark red smudge of blood. Treat your cat with a powder or spray.

Grooming Guide

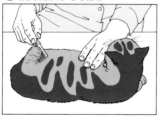

1 Use a metal comb with fine teeth to work through the fur, starting from the head.

2 Now turn your cat over and gently comb the fur on the underside and chest.

Around the Eyes

Your cat's eyes should be bright and clear. Any discharge or inflammation may indicate a health problem. To remove unsightly "tear stains," wipe around the eyes with a moist cotton ball.

Caring for Claws

Claws don't often become caked with dirt, but if they do, you can clean them using damp cotton balls. Trimming claws is tricky. Ask your vet to show you how to do it safely.

3 With a rubber brush, smooth the fur, working in the direction of growth.

4 Use a soft cloth, or a scrap of silk or velvet, to give a rich, glossy sheen to the coat.

Grooming Longhairs

Keep your longhaired cat looking absolutely immaculate with thorough daily grooming. Your cat will love the attention, and you'll be rewarded by a vision of feline splendor.

*T*OOTH CARE
Keep a check on teeth and gums. If necessary, the teeth can be cleaned with a soft brush and salt water.

*G*ROOMING GUIDE

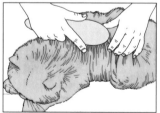

1 *Use a bristle brush to lift the fur all over the body and to remove any loose hair.*

2 *Next, brush thoroughly up and down, remembering to include abdomen and tail.*

*F*ABULOUS *F*UR
This Maine Coon steps out
regally, showing finely feathered
paws and a proudly plumed tail.

*E*YES AND *E*ARS
Delicate areas need special care.
Use a moistened cotton ball to
wipe away "tear stains" around
the eyes. Use a damp cotton swab
to cleanse the outer ear gently –
but don't probe too deep.

3 Use a comb to work gently
at any stubborn tangles or
knots in the luxuriant fur.

4 Finally, fluff up the fur
around the face with a
toothbrush for a pretty ruff.

PRIZEWINNERS

Is your cat champion material? There are numerous classes in which prizes are awarded in shows held every year. Non-pedigrees can enter too, and may win on the strength of charm and personality.

Show Time

Don't subject a timid cat to the rigors of the show ring, even if you think you own the most beautiful specimen ever born. Show cats are handled during judging and must feel perfectly at ease when being picked up and examined by total strangers. Your cat must put up with inquisitive human faces peering into the cage – heaven for an extrovert Siamese, but purgatory for a timorous Russian Blue.

Peak Condition

Longhaired cats should have the fur fluffed out on body and face for showing purposes.

WELL PREPARED

Regular grooming in the weeks leading up to the show, plus a good and varied diet, will ensure that puss is in top form on the day. Make sure that vaccinations are up-to-date in good time, otherwise your cat will not be allowed to compete.

POINT SCORES

Entrants must match up to the standard set for their breed, covering condition; texture and color of coat; shape of the body, head, and tail; and shape and color of the eyes.

CAT ACCESSORIES

A few simple items of basic equipment are all your cat needs in order to be a warm, comfortable, and happy member of the household.

PERSONAL PROPERTY

It's not essential to provide your cat with her own bedding and toys, but you can be sure that if you don't, she will start to improvise by snoozing on your best chair or by playing with delicate houseplants.

DINNER TIME

A dish for food, with a separate container for water, is vital.

FINE FARE

Uneaten food must not sit around and become stale. Remove any untouched food after half an hour. Wash the bowl thoroughly before the next meal. Place your cat's feeding bowl on newspaper to avoid any mess on the floor.

PRIVATE BATHROOM

A hooded litter box with a carbon-fiber filter to minimize unpleasant odors is the height of feline luxury. Cats appreciate a little privacy, especially in a small or crowded home.

UP TO SCRATCH

If your cat starts to sharpen her claws on the furniture, say "no" firmly. Then carry her over to the scratching post. Attaching a small toy to the post may make it more attractive to feline eyes, and some posts are impregnated with catnip to make them more alluring.

TREATS FOR YOUR

Cat

*Pamper your feline friend
with very special meals,
body massage, and lots of
fun and games!*

SENSUOUS DELIGHTS

These sublime treats will soon have your cat purring.
Cats enjoy such pleasures as catnip planted in the sun
or a pot of lush green grass to nibble.

DELECTABLE SCENT
Plant a patch of catnip
(*Nepeta cataria*, also
called catmint) in a
sunny spot. Oils in
the leaves contain a
chemical component
that sends sensitive cats into a
state of bliss. Cats roll on the
plant, releasing the aroma.

SUCCULENT SNACK
Grass contains valuable vitamins
and helps cats to regurgitate
hairballs. Chewing grass is not
a sign that your cat is ill.

BEDTIME BLISS
Cats like to stretch out, so choose
a basket that is big enough. Line it
with an old blanket, or, for total
luxury, use a lamb's fleece.

BODY MASSAGE
Wait until your cat is on your lap
and in the mood for stroking,
then begin a gentle "massage."
Using both hands, stroke firmly
from shoulder to
rump, caressing her
spine and sides.
Then scratch
gently behind the ears
and on top of the head. Stroke
under the chin with your index
finger and listen to the purrs!

GOOD COMPANIONS
Human company is vital
to cats. They can
become unhappy and
introverted when they
feel neglected. Consider
taking two kittens from
the same litter, as they
will keep each other
entertained when you
have to go out.

GAMES AND PLAY

Play is a very important part of a cat's life. It's fun –
and cats are devoted to having fun – it's a good way of
getting exercise, and it provides an opportunity
to practice stalking, chasing, and pouncing.
Most cats will play happily on their own,
but are even happier if their owner can
find time for a daily play session.

CATCH AS CAT CAN
*Cats often pounce on
likely looking objects,
just to see if they make
good playthings.*

Good Games

Small objects that can be pulled along, or swung in the air, are ideal for pouncing games. Tweak the bait gently, to alert the cat's interest, then just as she's about to pounce, twitch out of reach.

Exercise Time

Bowl a ping-pong ball along the floor, flick pellets of paper into the air, or arrange a newspaper in an upturned "V" to make an inviting hiding place.

Favorite Toys

Pet shops offer a wide choice of feline toys, or you can improvise and make your own at home.

Jump for Joy

Any toy scented with catnip will have extra appeal for frisky felines.

TREATS TO EAT

Every cat enjoys a delicious little morsel prepared specially for feline consumption. While basic cat foods contain all the protein and vitamins needed to sustain your cat, these gourmet treats are guaranteed to tempt the most jaded palate – they are also highly nutritious and will keep your cat in the absolute peak of condition.

Breakfast Delight

Set your cat off to a great start each morning with a small portion of oatmeal made with warm milk or a mixture of milk and water. Allow the oatmeal to cool in a shallow dish, and serve at room temperature with a teaspoonful of cream on very special occasions.

Sweet Treat

Many health-conscious cats enjoy a little helping of plain yogurt, served just as it is. A thin trickle of honey over the top will be greatly appreciated by some cats. Unflavored, plain, low-fat yogurt is just as delicious, if your cat is at all inclined to put on weight.

Cheesy Fish Supper

Bake fillets of flounder or scrod in foil with a little milk for 15 to 20 minutes. Flake the fish, removing bones. Add the cooking liquid, top with finely grated cheese, and broil lightly. Serve cooled.

Speedy Snack

For a quick, filling meal, mash sardines that have been canned in oil. This treat is good for longhaired cats: the oil helps to ease hairballs through the digestive system.

Celebration Feast

Save the turkey giblets and simmer them gently for about half an hour. Dice the flesh with a few choice pieces trimmed from the bird. Serve moistened with the delicious cooking liquid.

Puss's Pasta

Cook macaroni for 12 minutes until tender. Simmer lean ground beef in a savory stock for 20 minutes. Combine the meat and macaroni. Cool before serving with grated cheese.

Sublime Soup

For a luscious consommé, simmer meat trimmings and bones in water for an hour, then strain through a fine sieve. A little chopped meat can be added, if liked.

Hearty Beef Stew

Chunks of stewing steak, pressure cooked for 20 minutes in a tasty stock, make a warming supper. Combine the stew with mashed potatoes or rice. Serve when cool.

Menu Planning

Cats enjoy a varied diet. Like humans, they get bored
if faced with the same food, day in and day out.

Canned Food

Canned pet foods give your cat
all the necessary nutrients,
although you can mix in some
dry food to give added crunch.
Do not give dry food on its
own, as it is low in fat and can
cause kidney problems. An
average-sized cat needs around
three-quarters to a whole can of
food per day, divided into two
or three meals. Keep opened
cans covered and refrigerated. A
few seconds in the microwave
brings food up to room
temperature. Cats don't enjoy
chilled food.

Fresh Meat and Fish

Try meals of raw ground meat (but not pork
or offal, which must *always* be cooked). Pour
savory juices over the meat before serving. Don't
give liver more than once a week. Beware of
splintery bones in chicken. White or oily fish,
lightly cooked, flaked, and with the bones
removed, remains a favorite feline food. Canned
sardines are a quick and convenient
meal – and highly nutritious.

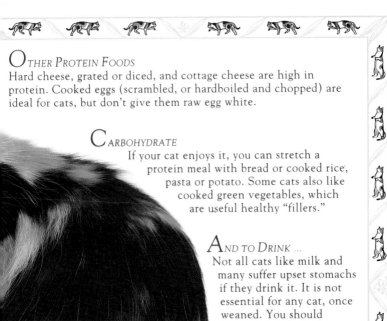

OTHER PROTEIN FOODS

Hard cheese, grated or diced, and cottage cheese are high in protein. Cooked eggs (scrambled, or hardboiled and chopped) are ideal for cats, but don't give them raw egg white.

CARBOHYDRATE

If your cat enjoys it, you can stretch a protein meal with bread or cooked rice, pasta or potato. Some cats also like cooked green vegetables, which are useful healthy "fillers."

AND TO DRINK ...

Not all cats like milk and many suffer upset stomachs if they drink it. It is not essential for any cat, once weaned. You should always provide fresh, clean water, although your cat may decide that he prefers puddles, dripping taps, and the contents of flower vases! Some cats dislike the taste of chlorine in tap water, but will happily lap at bottled, still mineral water. Your cat may even appear to drink nothing at all. Don't worry about this; cats survive happily with very little liquid.

Cat

FACTS

A treasury of vital information to enhance your cat's health and happiness.

MY CAT'S HEALTH AND HISTORY

🐾

My cat's name ....

Date of birth ....

Birthplace ....

Sex ....

Color of eyes ....

Color of coat ....

Weight ....

Food favorites and hates ....

....

....

CAT CARE RECORD

🐾

Dates of first vaccinations against:

Feline influenza ....

Feline infectious enteritis ....

Annual booster due every ....

Worming tablets given ....

Birth of first litter ....

Number of kittens ....

Date neutered ....

Name, address, and phone number of vet:

....

....

Dates of visits to the vet, and treatments prescribed:

....

....

....

....

Preferred cat sitters ....

....

....

Preferred catteries ....

....

....

CAT STARS

Pamper your cat according to the stars.

A_{RIES}
MARCH 21 – APRIL 20

Arien cats like to be out and about, tree-climbing and leaf-chasing; they are not pets for apartment-dwellers. They have masses of energy and lots of love to give. Keep your Arien female in when she's in heat, as this sign is renowned for its passionate nature.

T_{AURUS}
APRIL 21 – MAY 21

Every evening, on the stroke of feeding time, Taurean cats will be standing impatiently by their bowls. They cling to routine and adore their food. Don't give in to cries for "More!" At heart Taureans are country cats that like to roam the fields, chasing butterflies.

G_{EMINI}
MAY 22 – JUNE 21

Although Geminian cats hate being left alone, they don't make very restful companions. Brimming with nervous energy, Geminians jump at the slightest noise and are constantly on the prowl. Then they need lots of sleep, so provide a snug, warm bed.

C<small>ANCER</small>
J<small>UNE</small> 22 – J<small>ULY</small> 22

Cancerian cats can never get enough
affection; they positively adore being stroked
and cuddled. Cats born under this sign are
very emotional and don't respond well to
change or upset. They may suffer from
stomach problems, unless life remains calm.

L<small>EO</small>
J<small>ULY</small> 23 – A<small>UGUST</small> 23

Keep your wits about you if you own a Leo
cat, as this is the daredevil sign that will
creep up and steal your supper. Leos are very
lovable, though, and are always forgiven.
They are happiest in company and adore the
companionship of another live-in cat.

V<small>IRGO</small>
A<small>UGUST</small> 24 – S<small>EPTEMBER</small> 22

Simple pleasures of life (fresh fish and a
gentle brushing for a treat) make Virgoan
cats very happy. They don't like rich food
and shun too much fuss. Neat eaters, they
spend hours in fastidious washing before
curling up contentedly in their tidy beds.

*L*IBRA
SEPTEMBER 23 – OCTOBER 23

Libran cats drive their owners mad with their indecision. Do I want a lap? Or shall I settle on the chair? Would I like some milk? Do I want to come in? Or go out? Librans can never make up their minds, but at heart they truly are comfort-loving cats.

*S*CORPIO
OCTOBER 24 – NOVEMBER 22

Scorpios love rough and tumble and will enjoy strenuous games. They'll even let you rumple their fur, as long as you don't overdo it. Beware the Scorpio cat's jealous nature, and don't be seen fondling another cat unless you want to be ignored for at least a week.

*S*AGITTARIUS
NOVEMBER 23 – DECEMBER 21

Put your best china well out of reach if you own a Sagittarian cat. Despite their natural feline grace and agility, these highly active, boisterous cats can create havoc in the home. Sagittarians are happiest left to roam free, but they always return after their adventures.

Capricorn
DECEMBER 22 – JANUARY 20

Shy of showing their feelings, Capricornians need to be coaxed onto your lap. Once there, they will accept all the love and affection you can give them. They sometimes neglect their appearance, so make sure that longhaired Capricornians are groomed regularly.

Aquarius
JANUARY 21 – FEBRUARY 18

You never know what's going to happen next with Aquarian cats. One day they'll follow you around lovingly, the next they won't want to know you at all. Aquarians value their independence intensely, so don't thwart an Aquarian unless it's quite unavoidable.

Pisces
FEBRUARY 19 – MARCH 20

Dreamy Pisceans sit for hours gazing into the fire, lost in a world of their own. They are hypersensitive and hate sudden noises and people with loud voices – anything, in fact, that disturbs their reverie. They are adorable, affectionate pets. And, yes, they love fish.

A-Z of Health and Safety

A IS FOR AGE
Most cats age gracefully, but watch for appetite changes or weight loss, which point to the beginning of health problems.

B IS FOR BREEDING
Keep your pedigree female indoors when in heat. Make arrangements with a breeder for her to be served by a fine recognized male.

C IS FOR CARS
Many cats complain loudly when traveling by car, but in a safe, comfortable carrier, no harm will come to them. Provide water, food, and a litter box on any long journey.

D IS FOR DISEASE
Watch out for warning symptoms such as a cough or cold, sickness, lassitude, or change in appetite.

E IS FOR ELECTRICITY
Cats like to gnaw at plugs and wires. Prevent accidents by unplugging electric appliances when they are not in use.

F IS FOR FIREWORKS
Fun for humans, but terrifying for cats. Keep your cat safely indoors when the pops, bangs, and whizzes begin.

G IS FOR GARAGE
Forbidden territory for cats, who may lick up a puddle of antifreeze or spilled oil, with disastrous results. Check the garage or garden shed if your cat is missing. She may have dashed inside when you last opened the door.

H IS FOR HAIRBALLS
Hairballs can become a problem for longhairs, so regular and thorough grooming by you is essential to health.

I IS FOR INJECTIONS
Vaccination in kittenhood and annual boosters protect feline lives.

J IS FOR JITTERS
Nervous cats hate visiting the vet, and can be exceptionally hard to handle. Wrapping the whole body in a towel, leaving the head free, restrains the cat and helps to calm him. Talk reassuringly before, during, and after such restraint.

K IS FOR KITCHEN
A room full of dangers for inquisitive felines. Hot plates, gas burners, and ovens can all give nasty burns. Sharp knives should be kept safely in a drawer beyond paw's reach.

L IS FOR LIPS
If your cat curls back his lips in a grimace, he is showing a feline characteristic called "flehming." The cat reacts to exciting scents by making this strange, snarling face.

M IS FOR MEDICINES
To administer a pill, hold the cat firmly and grasp the sides of the mouth with your thumb and forefinger. Bend the head back gently and at the same time press the jaws gently so that the mouth opens wide. Drop the pill onto the back of your cat's tongue, then hold her mouth shut until you are quite certain that she has swallowed all her medicine.

N IS FOR NURSING
If your cat does fall ill and needs to be cared for at home, make sure that there is a warm and comfortable bed ready. A hot-water bottle wrapped in a blanket, or a heated pad, is always very comforting. Feed a light and tempting diet and do not allow the cat to go outside until she has recovered completely. Never give aspirin to a cat that is sick or in pain. It could kill.

O IS FOR OUTDOOR LIFE AND LEISURE

Allow your cat access to the outside world if at all possible. Cats will enjoy the exercise and fresh air, the chance to socialize with other cats, and a snooze in the sun. Nibbling grass is another healthy outdoor pastime.

P IS FOR PARASITES

Infestations of fleas are common, particularly in summer. Treat with a powder or spray.

Q IS FOR QUIET

Cats hate loud noises and hide themselves away from raucous parties or pulsating music. Respect your cat's need for peace and don't force him to endure noise.

R IS FOR REPRODUCTION

Kittens are adorable, but before allowing your cat to produce a litter, be sure that she is in good health. Remember that you will need to find good, caring homes for all the kittens, and be on hand to give several meals a day when they are very young.

S IS FOR SPAYING

Female cats can have this simple operation any time after the age of four months but not when in heat. Spaying involves the removal of both ovaries and much of the uterus under general anesthetic. It is a very safe, but irreversible operation with no aftereffects.

T IS FOR TOILET TRAINING

Introduce kittens to a litter box when they are three to four weeks of age and beginning to take solid foods. Give the box a permanent home somewhere peaceful where the cat can use it undisturbed. Regular cleaning of the litter box with detergent or baking soda is essential because fastidious cats may refuse to use a soiled box, and will choose a quiet corner in which to perform.

U IS FOR UNIDENTIFIED

A cat without a collar, to which a name tag is securely attached, could stray or be injured with no means for others to alert the worried owner. Most cats quickly adapt to wearing a collar, so make sure your pet never ventures out without one.

V IS FOR VET

Ask local cat-lovers or breeders for the name of a vet who is feline friendly. Choose a reliable practice that works extensively with small animals and that has a 24-hour service in case of emergency. Cats are usually extremely healthy creatures, but a visit is vital for booster vaccinations every year.

W IS FOR WINDOWS

An open window is like a magnet to a curious cat, but even sure-footed felines can fall and injure themselves. Shut your cat out when you want to air upstairs rooms.

X IS FOR XPLORING

It's in a cat's nature to wriggle into any inviting crevice or cranny. Cats can get trapped in drawers, closets, garden sheds, washing machines, and freezers, so keep doors securely shut.

Y IS FOR YOLK

Many cats enjoy cooked, chopped egg yolk on other foods as a treat. Give just one or two per week.

Z IS FOR ZAP

What your cat will do to any unwary bird or rodent who crosses her path. If you want a colony of mice wiped out, keep the cat well fed. Hungry cats lack the energy needed for serious hunting. Cats bring home prey and offer it as a special gift to their owner. This action is most common in neutered females who have no kittens to instruct in the skill of the chase. Try not to recoil in horror. Praise the cat for her generosity – and quietly dispose of the sad remains.

I N D E X

ACKNOWLEDGMENTS

Key: t=top; b=bottom.

All photography by Jane Burton except for:
Dave King: 8, 14-15, 17, 23b, 24

Fine Art Photographic Library: 10, 11t
Mary Evans Picture Library: 11b
Animals Unlimited: 12 • Daily Mail: 13t
20th Century Fox: 13b

Design Assistance: Patrizio Semproni, Camilla Fox, Ursula Dawson
Additional Picture Research: Diana Morris
Illustrations: Susan Robertson, Stephen Lings, Clive Spong